Searchlight
BOOKS™

Do You
Know the
Continents?

Learning about Antarctica

Christine Petersen

Lerner Publications ◆ Minneapolis

Content Consultant: Dr. Ryan Fogt, Associate Professor, Director, Scalia Laboratory for Atmospheric Analysis, Ohio University

Lerner Publications Company
A division of Lerner Publishing Group, Inc.
241 First Avenue North
Minneapolis, MN 55401 USA

For reading levels and more information, look up this title at www.lernerbooks.com.

Library of Congress Cataloging-in-Publication Data

Petersen, Christine.
    Learning about Antarctica / by Christine Petersen.
       pages cm
    Includes index.
       ISBN 978-1-4677-8023-0 (lb : alk. paper) — ISBN 978-1-4677-8345-3
    (pb : alk. paper) — ISBN 978-1-4677-8346-0 (eb pdf)
       1. Antarctica—Juvenile literature. 2. Continents—Juvenile literature. I. Title.
    G863.P47 2016
    919.89—dc23   2015001946

Manufactured in the United States of America
2-41945-18731-5/12/2016

Contents

Chapter 1

A FROZEN CONTINENT

Antarctica is the world's
coldest continent. Few animals
and plants live there. There are no
cities in Antarctica. The only people
there are scientists and other workers.
They travel to Antarctica by boat or plane.
They study the continent. Buildings protect
them from the harsh climate.

Antarctica has rocky, snowy landscapes. How do people reach Antarctica?

Antarctica was the last continent to be discovered. In the 1800s, hunters pushed south in search of seals. Finally, explorers first saw Antarctica in 1820. Their wooden ships were fragile. Ice trapped and damaged them. This made it difficult to explore. Modern airplanes make it much easier to visit Antarctica.

Sea ice made exploring Antarctica dangerous for sailors in the 1800s.

Covered in Ice

Antarctica is the fifth-largest continent. But little of its land is actually visible. Most of the continent is covered in ice. This ice averages 1.5 miles (2.4 kilometers) thick. About 90 percent of the world's ice is on this continent. The ocean around it is extremely cold.

Antarctica is far from the other continents. The nearest one is South America. It is about 600 miles (1,000 km) away. Antarctica contains the southernmost point on Earth. This spot is known as the South Pole. It is far from the coast. Traveling there was very difficult for early explorers.

Antarctica's ice extends in huge shelves off the edge of the continent.

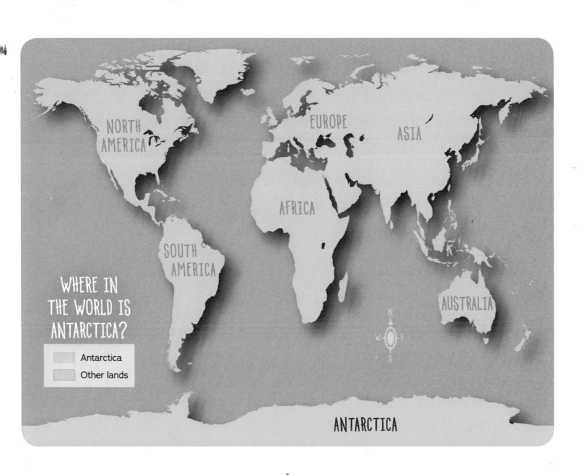

WHERE IN THE WORLD IS ANTARCTICA?

- Antarctica
- Other lands

NORTH AMERICA

EUROPE

ASIA

AFRICA

SOUTH AMERICA

AUSTRALIA

ANTARCTICA

ANTARCTICA COVERS APPROXIMATELY
5.5 MILLION SQUARE MILES
(14.2 MILLION SQ. KM).

Day and night last for months at the South Pole. Earth's tilt and spinning motion cause this. The sun begins to rise in September. It begins to set in March. Winter and summer are the opposite of what they are in the United States. Winter lasts from March to September. Summer lasts from October to February.

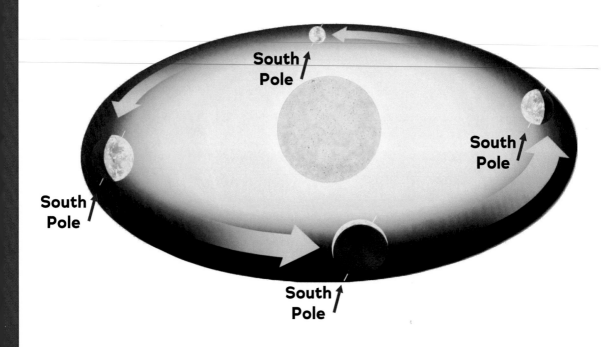

South Pole

South Pole

South Pole

South Pole

EARTH'S TILT LEAVES THE SOUTH POLE
IN DARKNESS FOR HALF THE YEAR.

The sun stays in the sky
for months at a time near
the South Pole.

Chapter 2

FINDING ANTARCTICA

Antarctica was discovered fewer than two hundred years ago. But people had suspected it was there for a long time. The ancient Greek scientist Aristotle watched eclipses. He saw Earth's shadow pass across the moon. Aristotle noticed the shadow was round. That meant Earth was shaped like a ball. He knew there was land in the northern area of the planet. He thought there must also be land in the southern area. Aristotle called this land Antarktos. This means "opposite of north."

Long before Antarctica was discovered, Aristotle thought there might be land at the bottom of Earth. What made him think this?

In 1772, British captain James Cook sailed south from the tip of Africa. He found thick fog and dangerous storms. Huge icebergs floated through the ocean. Cook turned back. He did not see a continent. But after his adventure, he said the area was so dangerous that no one could live there anyway.

COOK'S MAPS OF THE SOUTHERN OCEANS HAVE A
BLANK SPACE WHERE ANTARCTICA SHOULD BE.

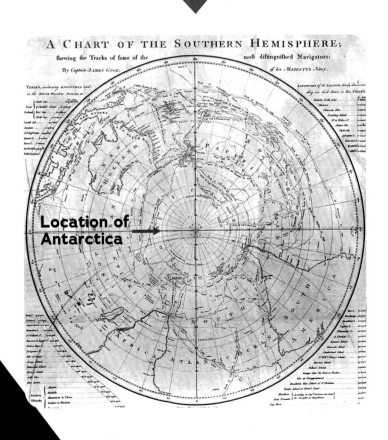

Early explorers relied on dogsleds to travel across Antarctica's vast, cold landscapes.

Countries in Antarctica

People began exploring the continent soon after it was discovered. Explorers reached the South Pole in 1911. They used dogs and sleds. In the mid-1900s, countries set up bases in Antarctica. These places were shelters where scientists could live and work safely.

In June 1961, twelve countries signed the Antarctic Treaty. This agreement said the countries would use Antarctica for peaceful purposes. They agreed to help one another study the continent. More countries signed the treaty over time.

MANY NATIONS HAVE SCIENTIFIC BASES ON ANTARCTICA. WHY DO YOU THINK MOST BASES ARE NEAR THE COAST?

▼

SANAE
(South Africa) ■

QUEEN MAUD
LAND

Showa Station
(Japan)

ENDERBY
LAND

Palmer
Station
(United States)

Halley Station
(United Kingdom)

Mawson
Station
(Australia) ■

EAST
ANTARCTICA

Bharati (India) ■

Amundsen-Scott
South Pole Station
(United States)

AMERICAN
HIGHLAND

ELLSWORTH
LAND

Vostok Station
(Russia) ■

WEST
ANTARCTICA

MARIE BYRD
LAND

Scott Base
(New Zealand)

WILKES
LAND

VICTORIA
LAND

ADÉLIE
LAND

THE REGIONS OF
ANTARCTICA

McMurdo Station
(United States)

Dumont d'Urville
(France)

■ Research station

Chapter 3

LANDFORMS AND CLIMATE

Antarctica is divided into two major parts. The larger part is East Antarctica. It is a huge plateau. It is the highest and coldest part of Antarctica. The smaller part is West Antarctica. The Transantarctic Mountain Range divides the two parts. The Southern Ocean surrounds the continent.

Scientists study Antarctica's mountains from the air. What mountain range is between the two parts of Antarctica?

The Antarctic Peninsula stretches out from West Antarctica. It looks a bit like an elephant's trunk lifted into the air. The peninsula reaches far into the Southern Ocean. It points toward South America. Many islands dot the ocean near the Antarctic Peninsula.

Ships must be tough to survive the icy waters of the Southern Ocean.

ANTARCTICA HAS SEVERAL MAJOR ICE SHELVES. WHY DO THESE SHELVES FORM IN BAYS?

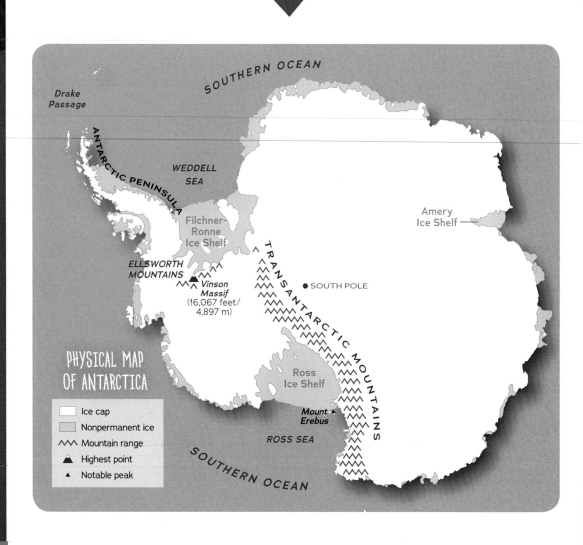

SOUTHERN OCEAN

Drake Passage

ANTARCTIC PENINSULA

WEDDELL SEA

Amery Ice Shelf

Filchner-Ronne Ice Shelf

ELLSWORTH MOUNTAINS

Vinson Massif (16,067 feet/ 4,897 m)

TRANSANTARCTIC MOUNTAINS

• SOUTH POLE

PHYSICAL MAP OF ANTARCTICA

Ross Ice Shelf

Mount Erebus

ROSS SEA

SOUTHERN OCEAN

- ☐ Ice cap
- ☐ Nonpermanent ice
- ∧∧∧ Mountain range
- ▲ Highest point
- ▲ Notable peak

Two huge ice shelves are attached to Antarctica. These are the Ross Ice Shelf and the Filchner-Ronne Ice Shelf. There is no land beneath these areas. The ice floats on the sea. Many smaller ice shelves lie along the coast.

Lakes and Mountains

Lake Vostok is in East Antarctica. It is one of the world's largest lakes. But it cannot be seen from above. It is hidden below 2 miles (3.2 km) of ice!

Most of Antarctica's mountains are covered in ice. Only the highest peaks rise above the ice. The tallest is Vinson Massif. It is at the southeastern end of the Antarctic Peninsula. The mountain stands 16,067 feet (4,897 meters) tall.

Temperatures in inland Antarctica are some of the coldest on the planet.

How Cold?

The coldest temperature in history was recorded in Antarctica. Russian scientists measured it in the winter of 1983. The temperature was –128°F (–89°C)! The coastal areas are warmer. In the summer, temperatures on the Antarctic Peninsula can rise above 50°F (10°C).

Most people think of deserts as hot and sandy. But some scientists call Antarctica a desert too. This is because a desert is any place that receives very little rain or snow. Only a few inches of snow fall in the inland areas of Antarctica each year. This would make it the world's largest desert.

Frozen Fossils

Millions of years ago, Antarctica was much warmer. Forests grew on the continent. Many animals lived there. Scientists have discovered their fossils in rocks throughout Antarctica. Scientists discovered that these fossils were similar to those found on other continents. This helped prove that the continents were connected to Antarctica in the distant past.

Activities thousands of miles away can have an impact on Antarctica.

Global climate change is affecting Antarctica. People burn fossil fuels to power factories and vehicles. Burning these fuels releases carbon dioxide. This gas causes the atmosphere to hold more heat. The climate becomes warmer over time.

This warming may cause some of Antarctica's ice to melt. Large ice sheets have collapsed into the sea. The changes can harm the continent's plants and animals.

SCIENTISTS IN ANTARCTICA STUDY THE CONTINENT'S AIR TO TRACK ITS CLIMATE.

Chapter 4

NATURAL RESOURCES

Antarctica's cold temperatures
make it difficult for life to survive.
The continent's plants and animals
are specially adapted to the climate.
Grasses and other low-growing plants live
on the Antarctic coastline. They can survive
long periods
of darkness
and cold.

Moss is sometimes found
along streams in Antarctica.
What is another kind of plant
that grows on the continent?

Huge colonies of penguins gather along the shore. The emperor penguin is the largest. It stands up to 4 feet (1.2 m) tall! Are you taller than an emperor penguin?

Each male emperor penguin keeps an egg warm through the long, dark winter. It balances the egg on its feet. The penguin mothers leave to go hunting. They return with food for their chicks.

Emperor penguins have thick layers of feathers and fat to keep warm.

On Islands and in the Seas

Small trees, ferns, and other plants grow on Antarctic islands. The islands are warmer than the mainland. Seabirds nest on island cliffs. Seals rest on the beaches.

The waters off Antarctica's coast are rich with life. Tall forests of kelp grow there. This underwater plant is food for small fish, snails, and starfish. Whales and seals swim through Antarctica's seas. They have thick layers of blubber to survive the cold water.

A TYPE OF BIRD CALLED THE SKUA FLIES FARTHER SOUTH THAN ANY OTHER BIRD.

Antarctic Krill

Krill are related to shrimp. These tiny creatures measure just 2.4 inches (6 centimeters) long. But they are very important to life in Antarctica's seas. Large sea animals, such as whales and seals, depend on krill for food. Millions of krill swim through the Southern Ocean.

Chapter 5

PEOPLE IN ANTARCTICA

In the mid-1900s, many countries set up bases in Antarctica. People learned how to survive the cold and darkness. Scientists from around the world work at dozens of research stations in Antarctica. Three of these stations are run year-round by the United States.

Bases give scientists safe places to study the continent. How many year-round bases does the United States have?

Argentina uses Orcadas Base, one of the earliest bases. Its people have been there since 1904. It is at the tip of the Antarctic Peninsula. The largest station on the continent is McMurdo Station. The United States set it up in 1956. More than one thousand people can live and work there. Scientists at McMurdo Station study rocks, weather, and many other subjects.

McMurdo Station is named for British sailor Archibald McMurdo.

McMurdo Station

McMurdo Station is like a small city. It has more than one hundred buildings. The station has a store, a post office, and a barbershop. There are buildings where people sleep, and there are laboratories where scientists work. A hospital and a church are available for residents. There are runways for planes and helipads for helicopters. The station even has a bowling alley and a gym!

The International Geophysical Year

In 1957, scientists around the world organized the International Geophysical Year (IGY). This was a period of time from 1957 until 1958 during which they cooperated in studying Earth. One thing they studied was Antarctica. The United States set up new stations for the IGY. So did the Soviet Union (a large former country made up of Russia and fourteen other nations).

THIS SMALL CAMP BUILT DURING THE IGY LATER BECAME MCMURDO STATION.

The Soviet Union built Vostok Station. It sits far inland in East Antarctica. Lake Vostok lies far beneath this station. Scientists at the station dig holes in the ice. They study the ice they find deep below the surface.

The United States set up the Amundsen-Scott South Pole Station. The base is located at the South Pole. Dark skies and clear air make it a great place for studying space. About 50 people work at the base in winter. This number increases to about 150 in summer.

Women in Antarctica

The first woman to visit Antarctica arrived in 1935. Her name was Caroline Mikkelsen. She came with her husband, the captain of a whaling ship. In 1969, American scientist Dr. Christine Müller-Schwarze arrived in Antarctica. She was the first woman to do research on the continent. Müller-Schwarze studied penguins. Many women, including Christine Schultz (BELOW) now do research in Antarctica.

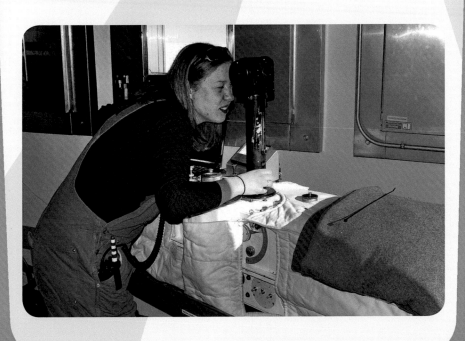

Chapter 6

ECONOMICS

The earliest explorers to reach Antarctica traveled there to make money. They were searching for seals they could hunt. They sold the seals' furs for money. Later explorers searched for valuable minerals to mine. They discovered that most of the continent was covered in ice. There was little exposed ground where they could dig for minerals.

Seal hunting drew people south toward Antarctica. How else did people try to make money on the continent?

PEOPLE IN ANTARCTICA DIG UP ICE TO STUDY
RATHER THAN MINERALS TO SELL.

▼

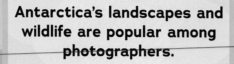
Antarctica's landscapes and wildlife are popular among photographers.

Tourism

The beautiful landscapes of Antarctica draw people to the continent. Thousands of tourists travel there each year. They come by boat or plane. They visit the continent to see its icy beauty. They take photographs of penguins and other animals.

Scientists worry about the number of tourists. Tourists must follow strict rules to keep the continent safe from damage. They must keep their distance from animals and throw away waste properly.

TOURISTS WHO VISIT
THE SOUTH POLE LEARN ABOUT
THE RESEARCH THAT GOES ON THERE.

Preserving Antarctica

Billions of people live on the other continents. Only a few thousand live in Antarctica. These scientists are learning more about our coldest continent. They study the land, the climate, the plants, and the animals. They work to preserve Antarctica for many years to come.

Studying Antarctica's landscapes and wildlife helps us understand Earth's coldest continent.

Exploring Antarctica

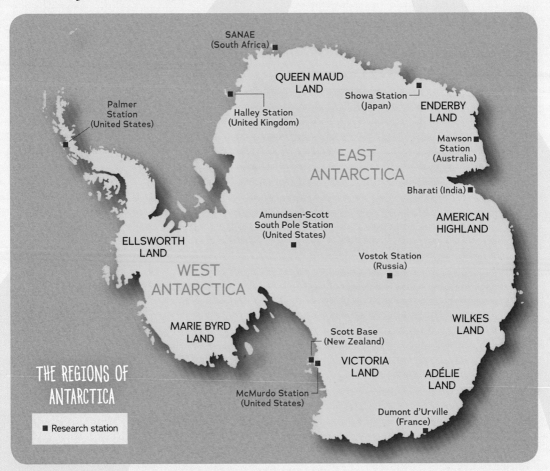

THE REGIONS OF ANTARCTICA

SANAE
(South Africa)

QUEEN MAUD
LAND

Showa Station
(Japan)

ENDERBY
LAND

Palmer
Station
(United States)

Halley Station
(United Kingdom)

Mawson
Station
(Australia)

EAST
ANTARCTICA

Bharati (India)

AMERICAN
HIGHLAND

Amundsen-Scott
South Pole Station
(United States)

ELLSWORTH
LAND

Vostok Station
(Russia)

WEST
ANTARCTICA

MARIE BYRD
LAND

Scott Base
(New Zealand)

WILKES
LAND

VICTORIA
LAND

ADÉLIE
LAND

■ Research station

McMurdo Station
(United States)

Dumont d'Urville
(France)

Choose a few places from the map that you want to
know more about. Research these places online. Write
a paragraph about a trip you will take to these bases.
What would you like to see and do there?

Glossary

atmosphere: the thin layer of gases that surrounds and protects Earth from sunlight

blubber: a layer of fat that keeps an animal warm

carbon dioxide: a gas released by some living things and the burning of fossil fuels. Too much carbon dioxide in the atmosphere can cause climate change.

climate: the long-term weather conditions of a place, including temperature and rainfall

eclipse: a natural event that occurs when one planet, moon, or star is hidden by another

fossil: the remains of plants or animals that lived long ago

fossil fuel: a substance formed from ancient plants or animals that can be burned for energy

peninsula: a piece of land almost completely surrounded by water

plateau: a high, flat area of land

treaty: an agreement between nations

Learn More about Antarctica

Books

Callery, Sean. *Polar Lands.* New York: Kingfisher, 2011. Read how creatures that live at Earth's poles survive in harsh conditions.

Friedman, Mel. *Antarctica.* New York: Children's Press, 2009. Check out this book to find more fun facts about the landforms, plants, and animals found in Antarctica.

Gogerly, Liz. *Amundsen and Scott's Race to the South Pole.* Chicago: Heinemann Library, 2008. Learn how explorers raced to be the first person to the South Pole in the early 1900s.

Websites

14 Fun Facts about Penguins
http://www.smithsonianmag.com/science-nature/14-fun-facts-about-penguins-41774295/?no-ist
See cool photos and learn interesting facts about penguins.

National Geographic **Education: South Pole**
http://education.nationalgeographic.com/education/encyclopedia/south-pole/?ar_a=4
Read more about the exploration of the South Pole and Antarctica and learn how today's scientists survive on the frozen continent.

Time for Kids: **Antarctica**
http://www.timeforkids.com/minisite/antarctica
Learn about how scientists work in Antarctica, read about shipwrecks and rescue missions, and discover how people use planes with skis to fly to Antarctica.

Index

Photo Acknowledgments

The images in this book are used with the permission of: Peter Rejcek/National Science Foundation, pp. 4, 14, 15, 19, 31, 35, 36; © North Wind Picture Archives, p. 5; Ethan Norris/National Science Foundation, p. 6; © Laura Westlund/Independent Picture Service, pp. 7, 13, 16, 37; © Dorling Kindersley/Thinkstock, p. 8; Marissa Goerke/National Science Foundation, p. 9; © Panos Karapanagiotis/iStockphoto, p. 10; © James Cook/Corbis, p. 11; US Navy/National Science Foundation, p. 12; John Evans/National Science Foundation, p. 17; Elaine Hood/National Science Foundation, pp. 18, 21, 26, 28; © M. Shcherbyna/Shutterstock Images, p. 20; Jenny Baeseman/Univ. of Colorado/National Science Foundation, p. 22; © BMJ/Shutterstock Images, p. 23; Jack Cummings/National Science Foundation, p. 24; Kyle Hoppe/National Science Foundation, p. 25; Reinhart Piuk/National Science Foundation, p. 27; Freddie Spainhouer/US Navy/National Science Foundation, p. 29; Josh Landis/National Science Foundation, p. 30; © Dmytro Pylypenko/Shutterstock Images, p. 32; © Vasilii Petrenko/Shutterstock Images, p. 33; © Keith Szafranski/iStockphoto, p. 34.

Cover image: © Planet Observer/Universal Images Group via Getty Images.

Main body text set in Adrianna Regular 14/20.
Typeface provided by Chank.